Contents

 Be considerate!

When visiting a place of worship, remember that it is sacred to believers and so be considerate to their feelings. It doesn't take a lot of effort – just attitude.

A Hindu priest during a festival

The Hindu mandir is a home

The Hindu mandir is a home for gods and goddesses.

HINDUS believe in one God. Hindus also believe that God has many different forms, and that worshipping one form of God is the same as worshipping all the forms of God. These different forms of God are represented by different **GODS AND GODDESSES**.

For example, the form of God that is responsible for creating wealth is the goddess **LAKSHMI**. If Hindus want to thank God for creating wealth, they would worship Lakshmi.

Every Hindu **MANDIR** is a home for one or more of the gods and goddesses. You would expect the home of someone as important as a god or goddess to look a bit like a palace. In fact, because **HINDUISM** began in **ANCIENT INDIA**, many Hindu mandirs are designed to look like ancient Indian palaces (pictures ① and ②).

For example, many Hindu mandirs have flags, called **DHAJA**, on top of them. In ancient times, Indian kings flew flags over their palaces, so the flags on the mandir remind Hindus that God is king.

▲ ② Hindu mandirs may have a carved gateway, to give a sense of awe.

▼ ① The mandir is just for worship, but there may be other buildings near the mandir that are used for community functions or for lectures.

Hindu mandir

Worship in the mandir

Lisa Magloff

Word list

Look out for these words as you go through the book. They are shown using CAPITALS.

ANCIENT INDIA Hinduism began in India around 4,000 years ago. Many of the customs and types of worship in Hinduism are taken from things done in the India of that time.

AARTI A type of worship where a fire is blessed by a god or goddess and then the blessed fire is shared by worshippers.

BRAHMA The Hindu god responsible for creating the world and everything in it.

CHANTING A type of prayer where certain words are repeated out loud in a rythmic way.

DHAJA The flags that are on the very top of many Hindu mandirs.

GANESHA The Hindu god of wisdom, education, knowledge and luck. Ganesha is one of the most important Hindu gods. He is often worshipped before any new project is begun.

GOD/GODDESS A representation of a form of God. Hindus believe that there is only one God, but that God has many forms, and worshipping a god or goddess is the same as worshipping all of God. There are many Hindu gods and goddesses, and they each have names, a unique appearance and many unique features.

HINDU/HINDUISM A Hindu is a person who follows the Hindu religion, sometimes called Hinduism.

HOLY TEXTS Ancient books which tell stories about the Hindu gods and goddesses. There are many ancient books telling stories, morals and teachings, and many of them are written in a language called Sanskrit, which was used when Hinduism began.

INCENSE A powder or stick that gives off a nice smell when burned. The smoke from the incense rises up, carrying blessings and good smells to the gods and goddesses.

LAKSHMI The Hindu goddess of light, beauty, good fortune and wealth. She also represents love and grace. Lakshmi is often worshipped by people hoping to achieve success, but Hindus believe she will not help anyone who is lazy or wants only wealth.

MANDIR The Hindu word for temple. The mandir is where Hindus come to worship together and is a centre for the Hindu community.

MURTI A statue or picture of a god or goddess.

OFFERING A gift made to a god or goddess. Common offerings include food, flowers and incense.

PRASADA Food which has been offered to the gods and goddesses. The gods and goddesses bless the food and it is then shared among the worshippers so that everyone can share the blessings.

PRIEST A person who has been specially trained to lead worship. A large mandir might have many priests.

PUJA A type of daily worship performed in the mandir.

SACRED Something which has special meaning or importance in religion or in worship.

SARI A traditional type of clothing for women that is common in India. The sari is usually made of a single, long piece of cloth which is wrapped around the body many times.

SHIVA An important Hindu god. Shiva is the god of destruction. Shiva is responsible for change and for shedding of old habits. Shiva also represents goodness and self-control.

SHRINE A throne for a Hindu god or goddess. Shrines usually contain more than just a chair – they often have walls or coverings to remind people of the importance of gods and goddesses.

SPIRIT Most Hindus believe that some part of the gods and goddesses enters the statues in the mandirs during worship. This part of the gods and goddesses is sometimes called the spirit or essence.

THRONE A chair or other place where an important person sometimes sits.

TILAKA A mark made from coloured paste that some Hindus wear as a sign that they have been to puja. It is also a symbol of Hinduism. The paste might be made from sandalwood, ashes or another substance.

VISHNU The Hindu god who preserves and protects the universe. Vishnu also represents mercy and goodness and is always peaceful.

Traditional mandirs

Traditional Hindu mandirs may be made of stone and be covered with elaborate carvings and artwork (picture ③). Some of the artwork shows scenes from the lives of the gods and goddesses, and some shows scenes of everyday life, nature, or important events in the history of Hinduism. All of these images help worshippers remember the **SACRED** stories they have heard or read.

Everything inside the mandir also helps us to understand that the mandir is a palace for gods and goddesses (picture ④). On the following pages we will go inside a Hindu mandir and see how.

▶ ③ Hindu mandirs are often covered with detailed carvings in stone. These carvings are placed all over the mandir, so that wherever you look your eyes fall on images of the gods and goddesses.

▼ ④ The inside of a Hindu mandir may also look like a palace, with carved pillars, artwork and decorations in marble or even gold.

Weblink: www.CurriculumVisions.com

Inside a Hindu mandir

Hindus believe that there is one God with many different forms. In a mandir, statues remind Hindus of the different forms of God.

A mandir may be a home for just one god or goddess, or it may be a home for many gods and goddesses (picture ①).

Inside the Hindu mandir there are statues and paintings of all the gods and goddesses that live in that mandir. These images are called **MURTIS** (picture ②). Each murti is dressed and decorated to show how important they are.

Hindus believe that the murtis in the mandir are not just wood or stone images of gods and goddesses. Hindus believe that when they worship, the **SPIRIT** of the gods and goddesses (and of God) is actually present inside the murtis.

Just like we cannot see God, we also cannot see the gods and goddesses. So, the statues simply make it easier to see what the gods and goddesses who live in the mandir look like.

▲ ② Murtis are decorated in a way that shows how important they are. This is why some murtis may be shown wearing crowns, fancy clothes and other things worn in ancient India.

▶ ① A traditional mandir. Traditional mandirs are designed so that the murtis of the gods and goddesses are in the centre. The main god or goddess of the mandir is in the very centre, under a peaked roof.

The arches and entrance hallway of the mandir gives a feeling of awe and of entering an important room.

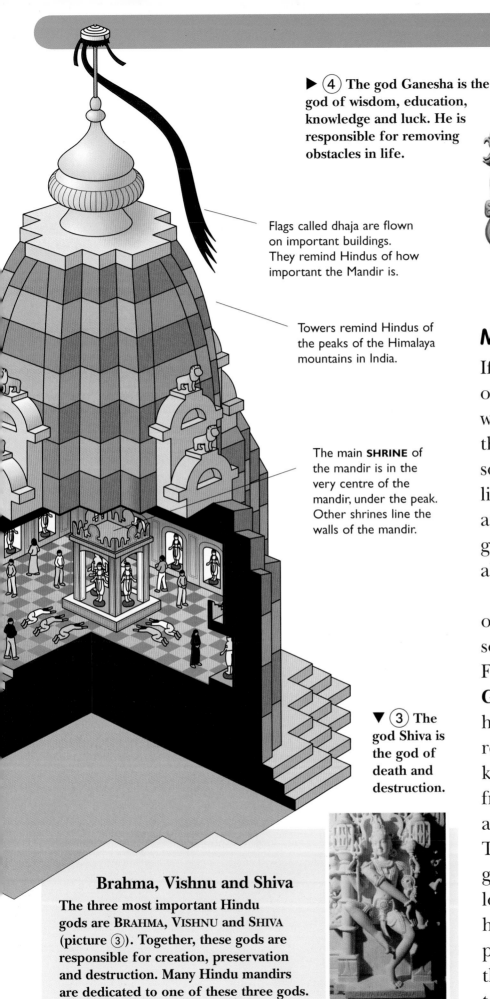

▶ ④ The god Ganesha is the god of wisdom, education, knowledge and luck. He is responsible for removing obstacles in life.

Flags called dhaja are flown on important buildings. They remind Hindus of how important the Mandir is.

Towers remind Hindus of the peaks of the Himalaya mountains in India.

The main **SHRINE** of the mandir is in the very centre of the mandir, under the peak. Other shrines line the walls of the mandir.

▼ ③ The god Shiva is the god of death and destruction.

Brahma, Vishnu and Shiva
The three most important Hindu gods are BRAHMA, VISHNU and SHIVA (picture ③). Together, these gods are responsible for creation, preservation and destruction. Many Hindu mandirs are dedicated to one of these three gods.

Many different shapes

If you look at the picture of murtis on this page, you will notice that some of them look like people, but some of them do not. Just like God can be anywhere and look like anything, gods and goddesses can also look like anything.

Usually, the way a god or goddess looks tells us something about them. For example, the god **GANESHA** has an elephant head (picture ④). This reminds Hindus that knowledge can be gained from listening (large ears) and thinking (large head). The position of a god or goddess can also tell us a lot. For example, if a statue has a hand up, with the palm facing out, this means that the god or goddess is telling us to be fearless.

Focus of worship

Each god and goddess who lives in the mandir has their own throne. These are the focus of worship in the mandir.

Thrones for gods and goddesses

Just like the mandir is a kind of palace home for gods and goddesses, each god and goddess in the mandir also has its own THRONE, called a SHRINE. The shrine may be carved out of stone, or made from wood or another material.

The shrines are usually designed and decorated to look like a throne for an ancient Indian king or queen. For example, the shrine may be covered with a canopy (picture ①) or have a carved throne chair inside.

Shrines may also be decorated with modern things like lights.

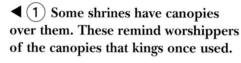

◀ ① Some shrines have canopies over them. These remind worshippers of the canopies that kings once used.

▼ ② The main god or goddess of the mandir lives in the largest shrine, which is usually in the centre of the mandir.

▲ ③ When Hindus worship, they go to each shrine in turn. Hindus may also worship at a particular shrine on their own, for example, if they want to ask a particular god's blessing.

Each shrine usually has a curtain or a door in front of it. This may be closed except when it is time for worship. Just like we need privacy sometimes, the gods and goddesses also like privacy, so the curtain is closed for some of each day.

In the centre of the mandir there will usually be a very large shrine (picture ②). This shrine belongs to the god or goddess who the mandir is dedicated to. The main god or goddess represents the form of God that is emphasised at the mandir.

The shrines, and the murtis inside them, are the focus of worship in the mandir (picture ③).

Showing respect

There are many ways that Hindus show respect for the gods and goddesses in the mandir.

How would you show respect to a god or goddess? You might start by taking off your shoes before entering the mandir, and this is exactly what Hindus do.

Because Hinduism is from India and most Hindus are from India, many also dress in traditional Indian clothes, like **SARIS**, when they visit the mandir (picture ①).

◀▼ ② Offerings to the gods and goddesses can be simple or very fancy. In the picture below, you can see that people have brought milk and fruit. In the picture on the left, the offerings have been arranged to look pretty.

▼ ① These women are showing respect by wearing traditional Indian clothes, called saris, to worship in the mandir.

Another way that Hindus show respect for the gods and goddesses is by bringing gifts, called **OFFERINGS**, to the gods and goddesses in the mandir (picture ②). These gifts might be flowers, food, **INCENSE** or even clothes. Some Hindus in the UK might offer things that are common in India, like coconuts and yogurt, while others might offer things more common in the UK, like apples and grapes.

Caring for the statues

The way Hindus treat the statues and artworks in the mandirs also shows respect. Statues may be washed daily and dressed in nice clothes and jewellery. Hindus may also show respect by bowing in front of the shrines (picture ③), or by circling around them while reciting prayers.

There are usually no chairs inside the mandir. This is because worshippers stand and walk from shrine to shrine when they worship. Just like you would not expect a god or goddess to get up and come to you, so the worshippers go to each shrine when they worship.

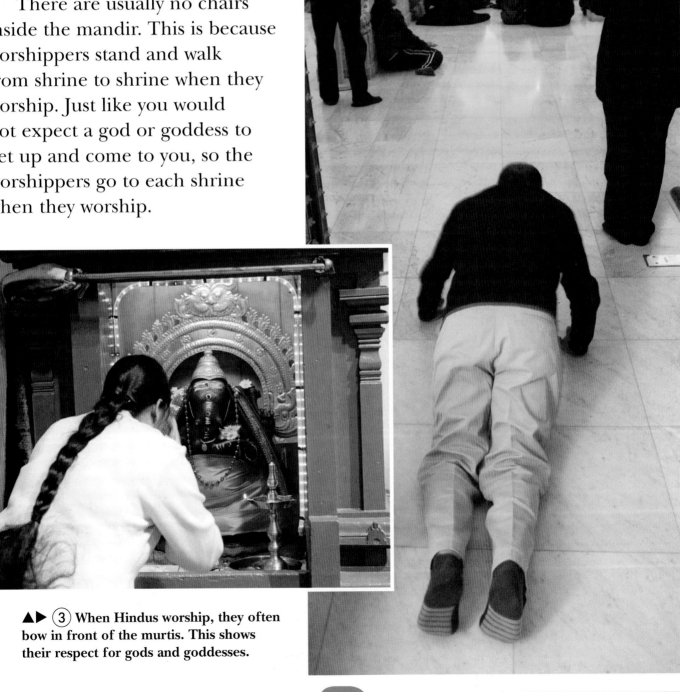

▲▶ ③ When Hindus worship, they often bow in front of the murtis. This shows their respect for gods and goddesses.

Daily worship

In the mandir, one type of worship is conducted every day.

Daily worship is one way that Hindus show love and devotion to God and to gods and goddesses. Another word for daily worship is **PUJA**. During puja, Hindus believe that the gods and goddesses come into the statues in the mandir. So, worship is a time for both honouring and communicating with the gods and goddesses.

Puja may be conducted by a Hindu **PRIEST**, but it may also be conducted by any adult who knows how. Worshippers and priests move around the mandir, conducting puja in front of each shrine in turn.

Honoured guests

During puja, the gods and goddesses are treated the way people in ancient India once treated very special guests, like kings and queens.

There are many ways of conducting puja, but the most common involves a certain sequence of events.

First, the god or goddess is invited to join the worshippers with **CHANTING** and prayers, and ringing a bell (picture ①). Once the god or goddess has arrived, they are treated like a very special guest. They are bathed and dressed and sprinkled with perfumes

Puja

A daily puja might involve all of the following things. During each step, prayers to the god or goddess may be spoken or chanted.

1. The god or goddess is welcomed with prayers and chants and offered a seat.

◄ ① The god or goddess may be invited to join worshippers with the ringing of a bell.

2. Using prayer, the god or goddess is asked about his/her trip to the mandir.

3. The feet of the god or goddess are washed with water.

4. An offering of water is made by sprinkling it around the shrine.

▲ ② Offering flowers.

while prayers are chanted. The god or goddess may also be offered flowers (pictures ② and ③), fruit, sandalwood paste, incense, chants and prayers or praise and gratitude. In some pujas, the gods and goddesses may also be offered music and dancing.

5. Water is offered to the god or goddess for washing his or her face and mouth.

6. A drink, usually milk, or milk mixed with honey or sugar is offered to the god or goddess.

7. The god or goddess is offered water for bathing.

8. The god or goddess is offered clothes and jewellery.

9. Sandalwood paste and grains of rice mixed with red colouring are offered.

10. Flowers are offered (pictures ② and ③).

11. Incense is lit.

12. A lamp is lit (picture ④).

▼ ④ A lamp is lit.

13. Rice, fruit, butter, sugar or other foods are offered (picture ③).

14. The god or goddess is bidden farewell.

▲ ③ Offerings of flowers, rice and sweet foods.

Personal puja

In the mandir, puja is often conducted five times each day – sunrise, morning, afternoon, sunset and at night.

Puja may also be held at other times and sometimes individuals or families may ask for a special puja to mark a particular event. For example, if a person starts a new business, they may ask for a puja to honour **GANESHA**, the god of wisdom, luck and success. Or, if a baby is born, the family may have a puja to ask the gods and goddesses to look after the baby.

Sharing blessings

After puja, there are usually two more types of worship. Each of these involves sharing the blessings of the gods and goddesses.

Hindus believe that whenever something is offered to a god or goddess during worship, it is blessed and filled with good energy from the god or goddess. So, after the puja ceremony, there are usually two more ceremonies in which worshippers can share the blessings of the gods and goddesses.

▼ ① **After the aarti ceremony, worshippers wave their hands over the flame and then over their heads, to share the blessing.**

Special lamps

Special lamps are used in a ceremony called **AARTI** (pictures ① and ②). The word aarti also means sacred flame, and during this ceremony a lamp is waved in front of each god and goddess while prayers are chanted.

Then, each worshipper waves their hands over the flame (not too close) and over their head. In this way, the god or goddess blesses the flame, and then each worshipper receives the blessing.

◄ ② Worshippers share in the aarti ceremony.

▲ ③ Sharing food that has been blessed by the gods and goddesses is an important part of worship in the mandir. Sometimes, for festivals and big celebrations, a lot of food is made by volunteers.

Sharing food

Another type of shared blessing is called **PRASADA**. First, food is offered to the gods and goddesses, who bless it. The blessed food is then shared by the worshippers, so that everyone can share the blessing (pictures ③ and ④). The food is usually something sweet, like fruit or rice pudding, to remind Hindus of the sweetness of God.

Sometimes, flowers are blessed by the gods and goddesses and then given to worshippers, as another reminder of the blessings of the gods and goddesses.

▼ ④ This food was blessed by the gods and goddesses of the mandir and is being shared among the worshippers.

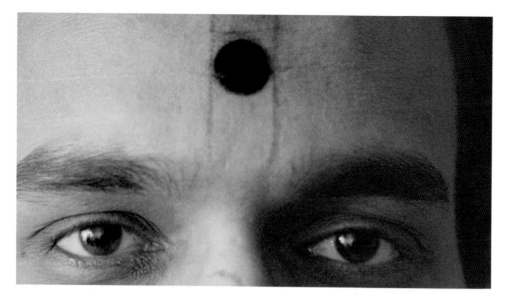

◀ ① Worshippers make the tilaka with coloured sandalwood paste that has been blessed by the god or goddess. There are many different shapes of tilaka. The most common is a single dot.

▼ ② Each person puts the tilaka on for themselves.

Visible reminders

In the mandir, many Hindus wear visible reminders of the blessings of the gods and goddesses.

Sacred marks

If you visit a Hindu mandir, you may see people with marks on their foreheads. These marks are made from coloured paste and are called **TILAKA** (pictures ① and ②).

The tilaka is put on after worship and stays on all day as a reminder that God is present with the worshipper throughout the day, and not just inside the mandir.

The tilaka is always put on the forehead, in-between the eyebrows. Most Hindus believe this is the part of our body where wisdom and concentration come from.

► ③ This Hindu priest is wearing traditional clothes from India while he conducts a ceremony at the mandir. You can see the white sacred thread.

Different shapes and colours

The shape and colour of the tilaka changes depending on which god or goddess the person has been worshipping.

For example, Hindus who worship the god Shiva use ash to make three horizontal lines across their forehead, and sometimes on their upper arms also. The three lines remind them that God is responsible for three very important things: creation, preservation and destruction.

When Hindus worship the god Vishnu, they make a U-shape on their forehead with a red or yellow paste. This mark reminds Hindus that God will protect them.

The most common mark is a red dot, which reminds Hindus that God created everything.

Sacred thread

Another visible sign of being Hindu is the sacred thread. Not every Hindu wears this, but it is usually worn by all the priests in the mandir (picture ③).

The thread is usually given to a boy during a special ceremony when he is about eight years old. The thread is worn during puja and is draped across the shoulder.

The thread has three strands woven together, which stand for the three duties of a Hindu adult: To promote knowledge and wisdom, to look after and respect your parents, and to be a good citizen.

Learning and giving in the mandir

The mandir is a centre for the Hindu community. It is a place of learning and helping.

▲ ① Learned priests or teachers recite ancient Hindu texts and discuss them in the prayer hall. This is one way that Hindus and non-Hindus can learn more about Hinduism.

The prayer hall

Some Hindu mandirs have a separate room or building called a haveli, or prayer hall (picture ③). There are no shrines in the prayer hall. That is because the prayer hall is not a place to be with the gods and goddesses. Instead, the prayer hall is used for performances of sacred songs and dance, called bhajan-kirtan, for recitals of **HOLY TEXTS** and as a place where people come to listen to talks or lectures about Hinduism by **PRIESTS** or other learned people (picture ①). The prayer hall may also be used for community events and festivals.

▲ ② These women are donating their time to make garlands which will decorate the gods and goddesses during a festival.

Giving

Giving is also an important part of Hinduism. Every member of the mandir community is expected to help others in some way. This may be by cleaning the mandir, helping to prepare for festivals (picture ②) and holidays in the mandir, organising projects to help others, or by donating something to the mandir.

▼ ③ Hindus gather in the prayer hall to listen to religious teachers talk about Hinduism.

Special days at the mandir

Festivals and special ceremonies are another important type of worship that happens in the mandir.

▼ ① During the festival of Maha Sivarathri, a large fire is offered to the god Shiva. Incense and other things are burned in the fire as offerings. Decorated coconuts are also offered to Shiva and prayers, chanting, singing and puja continue all night long.

Most of the Hindu gods and goddesses have special festivals in their honour. These festivals are dedicated to a god or goddess and celebrate a particular event in the life of that god or goddess.

For example, one of the most popular Hindu festivals is called Diwali. Diwali celebrates the killing of an evil king by Lord Rama.

Picture (1) shows the festival of Maha Sivarathri being celebrated in a mandir in London. This festival is for the god Shiva. It celebrates the time when Shiva saved the world by drinking a deadly poison. At this festival, offerings of fire and decorated coconuts are made, and special prayers are recited all night long.

Celebrations

Each Hindu festival is celebrated in a different way. Worship may include special prayers, singing and music. The statues of the god or goddess are usually placed on a special throne and paraded around the mandir, or even around the streets. This is an ancient way of showing respect to the gods and goddesses (picture (2)).

Sometimes stories about the gods and goddesses are acted out, and special food may be made. For example, the festival of Ganesha Utsav is dedicated to the god Ganesha. During this festival, worshippers give gifts of a sweet called ladoo to friends and family, because this is said to be Ganesha's favourite food.

▼ (2) **In many Hindu festivals, the gods and goddesses are paraded around the mandir on special thrones.**

Weblink: www.CurriculumVisions.com

Hindu mandirs around the world

There are Hindu mandirs in many countries around the world.

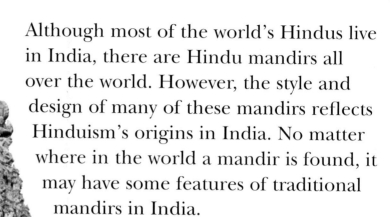

Although most of the world's Hindus live in India, there are Hindu mandirs all over the world. However, the style and design of many of these mandirs reflects Hinduism's origins in India. No matter where in the world a mandir is found, it may have some features of traditional mandirs in India.

Gopuram

Many Hindu mandirs have a tall tower over the entrance called a gopuram. The gopuram (picture ①) serves as the entrance gate to the mandirs and is covered with sculptures of gods and goddesses. As worshippers enter the mandir, the tall gopuram and its fantastic sculptures give worshippers a sense of awe and wonder.

◀ ① **This gopuram is at the Shree Meenakshi mandir in the southern Indian city of Madurai. This mandir is an important place of pilgrimage and it is estimated that as many as 10,000 people visit the mandir each day. There have been mandirs on this site for over 2,000 years, although the present mandir was mainly built in the early middle part of the 17th century.**

Mandir complex

Many mandirs are part of a large group of buildings called a complex (picture ②). The mandir complex may include many mandirs, living quarters for pilgrims and priests, kitchens, and sometimes even living quarters for mandir elephants.

Outside India

Hinduism was once widespread throughout South East Asia. In places like Indonesia and Thailand there are still many Hindus and many Hindu mandirs (picture ③). In these places, Hindu mandirs have somewhat different styles, which reflect the local culture. However, the mandirs still have many of the features of Hindu mandirs in India, such as gopurams, flags and offerings (picture ④).

▲ ② This large mandir complex is in Tirukkalikundram in southern India. It has a very large number of buildings to cater for all the pilgrims who visit each year. You can also see the four tall gopurams.

▼ ④ These Balinese Hindus are making offerings at the mandir. Hindus around the world do not always make the same offerings. Usually, they offer foods and other things that are common where they live.

▼ ③ This mandir is on Bali, in Indonesia. It is called Pura Besakih, the mother mandir, and it was built on the slopes of the mighty volcano Gunung Agung, which is a very holy place to the Balinese.

23

Index

Curriculum Visions

Curriculum Visions is a registered trademark of Atlantic Europe Publishing Company Ltd.

Atlantic Europe Publishing

Teacher's Guide
There is a Teacher's Guide to accompany this book, available only from the publisher.

Dedicated Web Site
There's more about other great Curriculum Visions packs and a wealth of supporting information available at our dedicated web site:

www.CurriculumVisions.com

First published in 2004 by
Atlantic Europe Publishing Company Ltd
Copyright © 2004
Atlantic Europe Publishing Company Ltd

Authors
Lisa Magloff, MA and Brian Knapp, BSc, PhD
Religious Adviser
BAPS Shree Swaminarayan mandir, Neasden, London
Art Director
Duncan McCrae, BSc
Senior Designer
Adele Humphries, BA

Acknowledgements
The publishers would like to thank the following for their help and advice: BAPS Shree Swaminarayan mandir, Neasden, London; Highgate Murugan mandir, Highgate, London.

Photographs
The Earthscape Editions photolibrary.
Illustrations
David Woodroffe
Designed and produced by
Earthscape Editions
Printed in China by
WKT Company Ltd

Hindu mandir – *Curriculum Visions*
A CIP record for this book is available from the British Library

Paperback ISBN 1 86214 414 1
Hardback ISBN 1 86214 416 8

This product is manufactured from sustainable managed forests. For every tree cut down at least one more is planted.